SMALL SPACES, BIG APPEAL

SMALL SPACES, BIG APPEAL

the luxury of less in under 1,200 square feet

FIFI O'NEILL

WITH PHOTOGRAPHY BY MARK LOHMAN

CICO BOOKS

LONDON NEW YORK

Editor: Sophie Devlin
Art director: Sally Powell
Production manager: Gordana Simakovic
Senior commissioning editor: Annabel Morgan
Creative director: Leslie Harrington

Photography: Mark Lohman
Additional photography: Sunday Hendrickson

For photography credits, see page 160.

First published in 2023 by CICO Books
An imprint of Ryland Peters & Small
20–21 Jockey's Fields
London WC1R 4BW
And
341 E 116th St
New York, NY 10029

www.rylandpeters.com

10 9 8 7 6 5 4 3 2 1

Text © Fifi O'Neill 2023
Design and photography © CICO Books 2023
ISBN: 978-1-80065-219-4

A CIP catalog record for this book is available from
the Library of Congress and the British Library.

Printed and bound in China.

Contents

INTRODUCTION

"'Mid pleasures and palaces though we may roam,
Be it ever so humble, there's no place like home."
—John Howard Payne

If there is a single trait shared by people residing happily in small homes, it has to be their resourcefulness. It allows them to organize and maximize even the smallest of nests while instilling charm, comfort and personality and embracing a more sustainable way of life. As the popularity of the Swedish philosophy of *lagom* (meaning "just the right amount") demonstrates, there is an art to living with less.

Contentment comes not in amassing things but in being selective about including only the most useful, beautiful and meaningful ones. Though the homes in this book are small, their owners have big dreams, which they have realized by choosing creativity over conformity. They understand that a compact space doesn't preclude a stylish aesthetic. What matters is the spirit they bring to their rooms and how they incorporate some of their existing possessions while letting go of others.

Small Spaces, Big Appeal captures the luxury of less by showcasing dwellings across a spectrum of styles and locations, all under 1,200 square feet/111 square meters. Each of these unique and imaginative homes offers inspiring interiors, ingenious solutions for compact quarters and stories of happy homeowners who have downsized their living space. Whatever your preferred look—nostalgic or modern, country, coastal or urban, minimalist or maximalist—it can be achieved within a small footprint.

Decorating with style, beauty and function is a question of how we use the space available to us, not its size. The process is a lesson in self-awareness, as it teaches us to reconsider our priorities, adapt to change, be disciplined, get creative and, ultimately, discover how even the tiniest of homes can meet our needs. The luxury of less is not only an attainable goal but also proves that good things do indeed come in small packages.

OPPOSITE: *Pairing a modern, slender console with a dazzling antique chair instantly transforms a blank spot into a small but chic workspace.*

RIGHT: *A translucent plastic material, originally used for agricultural buildings because of its ability to let the light in, has here been adopted for interior walls.*

FAR RIGHT: *Bins, cubicles and hangers keep clothing, shoes and files organized. Conveniently spaced shelves and a hanging rail make optimal use of vertical storage.*

Living in a small home calls for a much different approach than one would take in a larger space. Limited square footage requires a healthy dose of creativity and resourcefulness to achieve comfort and functionality while still allowing a favorite aesthetic. Many factors come into play when you are seeking solutions to maximize the available space. Understanding all the attributes and challenges of your home is the key to identifying how to make it work to its fullest.

SMALL-SPACE SOLUTIONS

SIZE MATTERS

One way to attain visual clarity is by sketching the floor plan on a piece of paper so that you can see the dimensions of each room, and then taking stock of the furnishings you already own. Consider whether the scale of each piece is appropriate for its setting and also how versatile it is. When you have limited square footage to work with, it is worth investing in multifunctional items—a table that can serve as a desk, a sofa that turns into a guest bed or stools and ottomans that double as side tables. Letting go of pieces that take up space inefficiently will make room for the right items, which allows the home to breathe and creates a sense of flow.

Custom built-ins can help you make the most of every inch of space.

LEFT: Set in a recess, a freestanding pantry cabinet and floating shelves answer a kitchen's storage needs without impeding on the floor space.

OPPOSITE ABOVE LEFT: When space is precious, it makes sense to carve out room for an eating area while making use of a redundant corner.

OPPOSITE ABOVE RIGHT: A custom-made curtain hung from a simple tension rod turns an awkward spot into concealed storage for boxes, baskets or suitcases.

OPPOSITE BELOW RIGHT: Making the most of available wall space, a floor-to-ceiling bookcase takes storage to the max and keeps tomes organized.

THE GREAT DIVIDE

In most small homes, spaces need to serve more than one purpose. A bedroom may become a home office during the day, a living room has to fit a dining table and a mudroom is also a storage area. One solution is to mark out zones using rugs and separate them with folding screens, bookshelves and even curtains.

STORAGE WITH STYLE

You can never have enough storage, but custom built-ins can help you make the most of every inch of space and keep everything neatly out of sight. A kitchen nook with a banquette, a window seat with a removable top and a trundle bed all provide clever storage solutions for a multitude of items.

LIGHTING

Good lighting is another essential part of making any room more spacious and welcoming, especially in smaller areas such as hallways, foyers and bathrooms, which often have tiny windows or none. Floor space is precious. While a well-placed floor lamp can make a nice style statement, so can a line of wall sconces or ceiling lights. For narrow rooms with high ceilings, pendant lights work wonders and draw the eye upward.

In kitchens, energy-efficient LED lighting above and under cabinets will maximize the room's functionality and is also the most sustainable choice. Don't forget hallways: low-profile wall sconces and recessed ceiling fixtures ensure a well-lit, inviting area. And remember to include dimmer switches for optimal ambiance.

No matter how small your space, proper lighting doesn't have to compromise on style or atmosphere. When you achieve the right balance of functionality and aesthetics, a small home lives large and feels downright perfect for its inhabitants.

OPPOSITE: *Slanted shelves and a simple over-the-door hook system bring additional storage with style and function to unused areas.*

ABOVE LEFT: *With many styles and materials available, hooks offer decorative appeal as well as practical possibilities.*

ABOVE RIGHT: *On a front porch against a background of weathered wooden shingles, farmhouse-style iron hooks are a suitably rustic choice for storing gardening gear.*

Despite or maybe because of their limited footprint, small spaces engender inventiveness, innovation and originality. By following a few simple rules, you can indeed bring maximum style to minimal space.

SMALL-SPACE STYLE

BANISH CLUTTER

Ask anyone who lives in a compact home what the number one step is in creating a successful small space and the answer is unanimous: editing. Visual clutter is enemy number one. That doesn't mean you have to embrace total minimalism, but be selective. Start by choosing a few statement pieces of furniture and art for each room, ditching bulky designs in favor of those with slender profiles. Then you can add a few well-placed accessories. Coffee tables, shelves and consoles make natural display areas, especially in neutral colors that keep the focus on the objects.

PALETTES AND PATTERNS

It is a well-known fact that light colors open up a room, while dark shades keep things feeling snug and cozy. Though a calm palette fools the eye into perceiving rooms as more spacious than they are, just because a home is small doesn't mean it has to be stark and minimalist. Incorporating a mix of shapes, textures and materials adds balance, depth and complexity to the decor and keeps it from looking sterile. If moody hues are your friends, try refining the palette to three main shades and playing with patterns and textures. And if you want to get the best of both worlds without fully committing to either, paint a dark color starting at the bottom of the wall and begin a more neutral shade halfway up to match the ceiling.

ABOVE LEFT: *A movable cart is ideal for a compact kitchen because it adds flair and convenience, and allows a great deal of flexibility in the layout.*

ABOVE RIGHT: *Cottage charm meets practical efficiency in the form of a weathered sign teamed with a stainless steel shelf with hooks for pots and pans.*

OPPOSITE: *Sticking to a light palette of white and wood and opting for open shelves is a no-fail aesthetic mix for small kitchens.*

ON REFLECTION

It is safe to say that when it comes to making a space feel bigger, brighter and lighter, nothing beats the optical illusion that mirrors create by bouncing light around the room. Oversize mirrors are especially dramatic in small rooms because they reflect the entire space, making it appear up to twice as large as its actual size. But even smaller ones will make a compact space feel more expansive by reflecting views and magnifying light.

EXPRESS YOURSELF

Even in a tight space, it is important to let your personality shine through in your choice of decor. Graphic paintings and prints, eclectic gallery walls and other artwork, such as typographic signs and textile wall hangings, tend to create strong focal points that deliver a powerful performance.

ABOVE: *Mirrors of all shapes and sizes, even a small one like this, add their unique characteristics to a space.*

LEFT: *Colors and shapes reflect the design influences that define this interior. Simple lines equate with modernity, while a palette of blues signifies a calm and serene environment.*

OPPOSITE: *Nothing says cottage style like a bedroom simply furnished with a vintage iron bed, nightstands/bedside tables, freshly laundered bedding and, of course, a sleeping kitty.*

Small spaces manifest their owners' desire for a simpler lifestyle.

LOOK UP

When floor space is limited, consider the vertical potential of your walls. Floor-to-ceiling shelving provides stylish storage to display your personal treasures and keep everyday essentials in order. Floating shelves and wall-mounted tables make wonderful alternatives to traditional consoles and nightstands/bedside tables—being able to see the floor creates the illusion of more space. Meanwhile, hooks and peg racks in hallways and unused corners house tote bags, hats and scarves at the ready.

LOOK DOWN

Hidden floor space under a bed or a sofa provides otherwise unused areas to keep flat storage bins, where you can stash extra odds and ends such as folded blankets, throws and bed or table linens.

Small spaces manifest their owners' desire to make the most of a simpler lifestyle by creating cozy sanctuaries focused on the elements they truly appreciate and the areas they use the most while exuding ease and individuality. Living small is living with thoughtfulness, intention and style.

The Homes

Going from a career in law enforcement to interior design might seem an unlikely move, but for retired federal agent Kim Kelly, it was a perfectly logical progression.

ORGANICALLY GROWN

OPPOSITE: *The new back porch addition was built to weather the elements and furnished to echo the natural beauty of its surroundings.*

ABOVE LEFT: *A vintage rug adds to the comfort of the interior. Kim found the sofas and tables in a consignment shop.*

ABOVE RIGHT: *The statement Broken Twig chandelier in the porch has always been part of Kim's home decor in all the places where she has lived over the years.*

Having needed to regroup from stressful and often dangerous days at work, Kim knew that coming home to a peaceful sanctuary was essential to her own wellbeing. She had already bought, remodeled and sold six homes over the years. "I always had a strong creative side and designing homes that reflected my personal style was important to me," she says. "I founded my company Bella Rustica Design Studio in 2008 and have been in business ever since. I found having a creative outlet was an excellent balance to the difficult investigating work I did as an expert in sexual assault, stalking and domestic violence."

LEARN TO LET GO

If you truly want to downsize your home, you will need to let go of items that don't support the new, simpler concept.

On her retirement, Kim was ready to downsize to give herself more options for traveling and new adventures, so she began looking for a small home that would meet her needs. "Two years ago, while trying to avoid a traffic back-up on the main road of St. Simons Island, Georgia, I drove by this house. It happened to be Open House Day, so I pulled over to take a look inside the little 700-square-foot/65-square-meter cottage. The neighborhood was safe and very walkable, which is important to me as a dog owner who enjoys walking as one of life's greatest pleasures. There was also easy access to shopping and to the road off the island. I made an offer and the deal was done."

TOP LEFT: *Juxtaposing the textures of water-friendly plants with geometric hard landscaping has created a garden with an organic yet modern sensibility.*

ABOVE: *Curtains contribute a cozy feel while offering privacy when needed. A secondhand dining table and chairs set the tone for convivial meals.*

OPPOSITE: *Kim feels strongly about living in harmony with the outdoors. A door from the master bedroom opens onto this large, private shower on the porch. The cow's head is vintage, from RH.*

OPPOSITE: *In the kitchen, Kim opted for eco- and pet-friendly carpet tiles from Flor made with recycled-nylon yarn. The work surfaces were made by Caesarstone.*

BELOW: *The front of the cottage bears its original façade. Kim added the modern address sign and mailbox and the dog statues that flank the entrance.*

RIGHT: *The cottage entrance is a welcoming space with a narrow table and benches, which fold up for easy storage and also come in handy for Kim to take to home-staging projects.*

Kim had big plans for the small home. "I bought it with the idea of adding a covered rear porch," she says. "The house doesn't have a dining room and the living room is quite small, so I wanted a spacious spot for entertaining." The cottage sits on a corner lot and the original address was on the side, and it seemed at first that the porch would not be allowed due to setback restrictions. However, Kim was granted a variance, which allowed her to build the 400-square-foot/37-square-meter addition that now runs across the back.

The previous owners had done an inexpensive remodel, but they had not updated the electricals and plumbing. The kitchen also needed some work to create more usable space, so Kim reconfigured the layout and moved the washer and dryer to a specially designed closet in the adjoining bedroom. This opened up enough room in the kitchen for her to install new custom cabinetry with concrete countertops. For the bathroom, she opted for a complete remodel together with modern fixtures and organic touches.

KEEP IT CLEAN

Closed storage cuts down on clutter. Go for suitable pieces (such as an armoire/wardrobe or a locker) that can hold and visually conceal a lot of items.

Kim's 15-year-old RH leather sofa wears its patina well. The wooden coffee table was handmade on site by the specialist local firm Island Sea Designs. This room also accommodates a small workspace and a metal locker that provides streamlined storage.

Living in a small space is liberating if one truly downsizes.

OPPOSITE: *In the guest bedroom, comfort is key. There are cushy pillows and crisp linens, plus a soft hide underfoot. Oversize art adds dimension and drama.*

RIGHT: *Spare blankets and throws are draped over a tall vintage ladder, which sets off the low modern storage cabinet from CB2. The round mirror balances their respective proportions.*

THE BIGGER PICTURE

Don't rule out larger pieces of furniture and art. It's all about getting the right visual balance.

Kim then shiplapped all the walls, added tongue and groove to the bedroom ceilings and painted the entire interior white. "Far from being boring or predictable, white provides a crisp, clean backdrop for most types of decor," she notes. "I have an organic, rustic-modern aesthetic and always include unique pieces of furniture when the space allows it."

Living in a small space is liberating if one truly downsizes, which requires a commitment to simplifying and a willingness to let go of items that have outlived their usefulness. "I sold everything that didn't fit the space, including several beautiful pieces," Kim says. She did hang onto her favorite leather sofa, which is 8 feet/2.4 meters long and 40 inches/1 meter deep. "I bought it 15 years ago and it is the most comfortable piece of furniture I have ever owned," she says. "Additionally, I have always had (and always will have) at least one dog—currently, Sugar, a rescued retriever-boxer mix—and leather upholstery is the best when you live with pets. The more patina, the better!"

Another treasured piece that made the move with Kim is her sculptural Broken Twig chandelier, which now plays a starring role in the outdoor living space. "It doesn't get more organic than that," she exclaims.

Aside from the required architect's plans for the back porch, Kim designed everything in this home and all her previous ones. Though she loves every room of her little cottage and how it lives large despite its small footprint, she is most proud of the outside porch. "It took a while to realize that once I retired from federal service, I could let my passion for design become a second career," she says. "Chasing down the perfect decorative elements is a lot less stressful!"

OPPOSITE: *Kim's less-is-more aesthetic continues in the bathroom. A wooden vanity is teamed with a simple basin and matte black penny floor tiles. The simple artwork is from Barloga Studios.*

THIS PAGE: *Textures and colors come together in the master bedroom. A bison painting by local artist George Netherton provides a focal point above the woven suede headboard. A faux-fur pillow and a pair of wooden lamps continue the warm neutral palette.*

Summer camp memories, artistic pursuits and her affinity for homes with a history inspired the decoration of Ellie Navarro's endearing cottage in North Carolina.

RURAL ROMANCE

OPPOSITE: *Old shutters, a makeshift sofa and a rescued table make the front porch a charming nook in which to read, take a nap or simply daydream. Ellie found the cow hide on Ebay and the artwork at Cottage Grove Vintage Market in Greenville, South Carolina.*

ABOVE: *Chairs inherited from Ellie's grandma, a salvaged table, a curvy chandelier and rustic sideboard set the stage for memorable alfresco dining.*

"I fell in love with the mountains as a child and always hoped I would be able to live here someday. When I was 25, I got my chance and moved from Georgia to Hendersonville, North Carolina," says Ellie. "I've always been hands-on, determined and curious, which led me to interior design and photography. My experience with building and remodeling homes proved to be very helpful when I bought this cottage as a single mom in 2007."

Since then, Ellie has been working to improve her 680-square-foot/63-square-meter dwelling while staying true to its origins. "It still has the original windows, the local granite stone fireplace and most of the antique oak floors, which were hidden under the carpet," she says.

THIS PAGE AND OPPOSITE: *Ellie revamped the kitchen by replacing the upper cabinetry with open shelving and the old work surfaces with new wooden ones. Painting the cabinets white helped to give the room a fresh new look. The lamp on the countertop came from the Antique Tobacco Barn in Asheville, North Carolina.*

I always embrace limitations that demand creative solutions.

ABOVE LEFT: *Organic materials, such as flowering branches in a wooden vase, are in keeping with the quaint, rustic nature of the cottage and its location.*

ABOVE RIGHT: *Simple fare and drinks take on an elevated appeal when presented in pretty dishes and glasses and served with a side of blooming persimmon.*

OPPOSITE: *In the little eating area, a table flanked by two chairs and dressed in one of Ellie's grandma's tablecloths nod to childhood nostalgia and heartfelt familial sentiments.*

"I pulled it up and discovered that there were holes in the flooring and subflooring. I could see the dirt in the crawlspace underneath—I'm not sure how I didn't step through to the ground. Thankfully, around 75 per cent of the floor was salvageable, but replacing sections was quite a project. I did most of the work myself, but I'm grateful for the friends who came along to lend a hand. I now know more about roofing than I care to, and I've learned that a good plumber is worth the money. The biggest challenge was not so much design as just elbow grease. It has been a really humbling experience for me."

Ellie describes herself as a problem solver, but a frugal one. "Whether I'm designing for others or for the cottage, I always embrace limitations that demand creative solutions, whether it be budget or other constraints. In the end, I think this approach produces better results," she explains.

USE RESTRAINT

Whatever your preferred aesthetic, stick with it. It will create harmony and cohesiveness in a small home.

THIS PAGE AND RIGHT: *The living room combines old and new in the form of preowned, slipcovered furniture, a modern coffee table from RH and accessories from the past, including Ellie's grandmother's sconce and vintage mirror. Touches of pink add cheerful notes, while black flooring grounds the space.*

BE FLEXIBLE

When faced with space constraints, take the time to rethink the items you want to include in each room. Even if you intended a piece for a specific place, this doesn't preclude it from functioning equally well in another one.

OPPOSITE: *Because the front bedroom doesn't have closets, Ellie constructed a built-in bed on a raised platform to allow for storage space underneath. The cupboard doors are attached with heavy-duty Velcro for easy access.*

ABOVE LEFT: *Pretty, new and vintage textiles in soft textures and colors, many of them collected by her grandmother, are intrinsic to Ellie's decorating style.*

ABOVE RIGHT: *Never one to pass up a good thing, Ellie rewired and repurposed this vintage chandelier, which had been salvaged from an old house in New York City.*

"I have a simple rule that I live by. Whenever I fall in love with something, I always ask myself three questions: is it functional, is it needed and is it beautiful? If it doesn't align with all three of those words, the answer is no. That helps me a lot!"

The front bedroom is a prime example of her ingenuity as a designer. Here, the problem Ellie faced was the lack of space to accommodate a large bed and a pair of nightstands/bedside tables. "Every arrangement of furniture that I considered for this space seemed awkward," she recalls. Her response was to reposition the doorway that leads to the adjoining bathroom—by doing this, she was able to free up enough room for a built-in bed. "It was the perfect solution, plus it allows for a massive amount of storage underneath."

Authenticity was another key concern. "I really tried to stick with the
cottage's vernacular," she says. In the kitchen, instead of investing in trendy
(and costly) granite countertops, she chose two slabs of wood and installed
them herself. She then replaced the upper cabinets with open shelving and
repainted the lower ones to give them a new lease of life.

She is also a fan of reconfiguring spaces. "We've had many bedroom
arrangements over the years. My daughter had a built-in crib, which later
became a bunk bed and finally a bench. All you need are a few screws,

some plywood and a can of paint." As for furnishings, she has a simple mantra. "Recycle as much as possible. Reusing and repurposing is better for our environment, and there's so much beautiful energy in older items."

Ellie acquired her love of antiques, patina and history via her grandmother. "She was very elegant and as a child I loved her home—it felt so timeless. My little home is really an homage to her. I think of her every day and honor her in my heart." No doubt her grandmother would be proud of Ellie's commitment to the cottage's roots, her sense of style and creative vision.

ABOVE LEFT AND INSET OPPOSITE: *Ellie built this bed out of plywood to fit the space. She also made the wall-mounted cabinet by attaching two old windows to a wood frame. The little bell hangs from a handmade leather strap. The wall sconce is from Anthropologie.*

ABOVE: *Shiplap walls and new fixtures and fittings bring the small but efficient bathroom up to date.*

Not everyone can visualize, and even fewer would be enthralled by, the potential hidden in a dated, run-down and borderline miserable 1950s cottage. But for Kristin Joyce and her husband Don Guy, this property in Florida was perfect. They had a vision.

NORDIC STYLE

When Kristin and Don's two grown-up children Lily and Jamison moved respectively to Brooklyn, New York and Oakland, California, it was time for the couple to downsize from their 2,500-square-foot/232-square-meter Sarasota home. Finding something in the same highly desirable neighborhood as their former home was paramount, but very difficult at the time. As fate would have it, this 1,050-square-foot/98-square-meter cottage suddenly came on the market as a rental.

SET THE SCENE

Create inviting exterior
landscaping to lead visitors into
a haven that, however small,
celebrates the luxury of less.

Not only was the property in their favorite neighborhood but it also offered a host of intriguing possibilities for its new tenants. Kristin and Don soon came to an arrangement with the owner so that they could make the necessary improvements to the run-down cottage. "Knowing that this would otherwise have to become a 'tear-down,' our landlord endorsed our makeover of the exterior and update of the interiors," Kristin explains.

Among the most notable issues she and Don faced at the start of the project were the old wallboards/plasterboard, 1970s ceiling fans, odd pass-through wall openings between rooms, chopped-up floor plan and overall lack of space. There was also no landscaping to speak of. None of these were a match for the couple's shared creative skills, however.

*White reflects all colors—
I love the calm it conveys.*

ABOVE AND FAR RIGHT: *A chic PVC rug from Chilewich is the foundation for the living-room decor. Natuzzi ottomans function as either footstools, extra seating or tables when topped with a tray. The mirror creates the illusion of a larger space, while floating shelves prevent visual clutter. A few of the smaller pieces were sourced from Pecky and Blu Home, both in Sarasota.*

RIGHT: *A modern narrow console and a keepsake carved wood chair create a stylish workspace behind the sofa.*

Kristin was a photo stylist and brand marketing expert in fashion and lifestyle goods for many years before obtaining her current role with Natuzzi Italia. She is one of the top US designers for the contemporary furnishings company, which is known for sustainable luxury design with an emphasis on visual harmony and fine craftsmanship. Meanwhile, Don has had an award-winning career as a director and cinematographer and, more recently, as a college film professor. All these experiences came into play in the metamorphosis of the once-derelict cottage into a sophisticated home that mirrors the couple's artistic abilities and aesthetic sensibilities.

"We covered every wall with white paint, filled in the odd wall openings to create more space for photography and artworks, added warm floor-to-ceiling lighting and updated some of the appliances," Kristin recalls.

ABOVE: *Open shelves let organized utensils and tableware become part of the decor. Cabinets finished with glossy gray paint bring contrast and definition to the mostly white kitchen, while the island adds workspace and storage.*

OPPOSITE: *A slim, portable storage cabinet keeps cookbooks, dishes and other essentials close at hand. A long, slender table from Blu Home is useful for a quick snack or as a work surface and occupies very little floor space.*

BE CONSISTENT

Bring together varying shades of white to make small spaces appear larger, then add bold accents to draw the eye.

OPPOSITE: Once a catch-all space off the kitchen, the dining room now offers a small but elegantly furnished corner. The Natuzzi leather chair can be moved to function as extra seating in the bedroom or living room when necessary.

"We also designed a dual-purpose work and living space, found storage solutions, masked dated tile floors with chic area rugs and uncovered a dingy porch to create a splendid sunroom." Her Danish heritage and Don's discerning eye are evident throughout the house, she explains. "In essence, we've ended up with a Nordic nest with a spacious, almost spa-like atmosphere, which reflects our mutual love and affinity for contemporary yet eclectic Scandinavian-inspired design."

Kristin's sense of *hygge*, the Danish ideal of warm coziness, has been a major influence on her lifestyle and decor choices. She strives to create a haven of calm where elements of comfort cohabit with simple beauty.

ABOVE: The narrow dining room called for specifically sized and carefully placed pieces. The round dining table, which was custom-made by Weatherend, unites with the clean, modern lines of the Parsons chairs to offset the feeling of confinement that might otherwise be created by the rectangular space.

"White, as we know, reflects all colors," she says. "I love the calm it conveys and the palette it provides—it highlights sculptural shapes and makes a wonderful backdrop for art. Depending on the room, the white-on-white palette may be accented with watery hues in pillows/cushions and throws, high-contrast iron, glossy cabinets or cognac-hued wood furnishings."

ABOVE: *In lieu of nightstands/bedside tables, floating shelves provide surfaces for essential items, such as a pair of lamps from Louis Poulsen, without taking up any floor space. The artwork on the wall is by Andrea Dasha Reich.*

ABOVE RIGHT: *A large armoire/wardrobe that Don designed with a yacht builder many years ago in San Francisco yields generous clothing storage. Its sleek and modern feel is perfectly suited to its new home in Florida.*

Kristin and Don have been married for four decades and have four grown children and two grandchildren, so there is a strong emphasis on family in their home. Most walls feature art, children's drawings or photographs. The latter, often in black-and-white or sepia tones, highlight Don's work and are the focus in several rooms, where they provide the only "colour," so to speak.

OPPOSITE AND THIS PAGE: *The spare room serves dual purposes as a home office and guest quarters, and is furnished to work as one or the other accordingly. The Pottery Barn bed was selected for its integrated storage compartments and the desk for its space-saving size.*

The end results of Kristin and Don's joint efforts speak for themselves, but so do the lessons learned along the way and the lifestyle philosophy they have embraced. "Cramped spaces require the ability to visualize and 'expand the eye,'" Kristin concludes. "But the biggest challenge is knowing how to do just enough, which is a good value to develop in this world."

MAKE IT YOURS

Think of ways to make your rooms feel authentic and original with personal touches such as family art, photography and meaningful objects.

THINK BIG

Don't shy away from including a couple of larger pieces. They will take a small space to a whole new level.

Former antiques dealer Katy Halligan can't pass up a good deal, and her love affair with pieces of the past is alive and well in the unique home she and her husband Will built in Fayetteville, Texas.

TEXAS PRIDE

OPPOSITE: *Modern recliners are juxtaposed with a vintage fire surround, creating an inviting spot and bringing stylish comfort to the open-plan living space. The small cow adds a whimsical touch.*

ABOVE LEFT: *An old hardware-store cabinet with many cubbies stands ready to corral and display smaller items.*

ABOVE RIGHT: *Affectionately named "Hank" the steer head takes pride of place as a favorite find and a state symbol.*

For over 15 years, the Halligans traveled all over the country in search of vintage and antique pieces to sell in their shop and at shows. "Texas was always fun to shop," Katy says. "So many fabulous items end up there. We met and made lifelong friends during these trips." The couple fell in love with Fayetteville and the surrounding area. It didn't hurt that the small town was within 10 miles of the iconic Round Top Antiques Fair, where dealers offer unique goods from around the world. Three times a year, during the winter, spring and fall fairs, the population of Round Top swells from a mere 90 to over 100,000. It is a fact that didn't go unnoticed by Katy and Will when they were contemplating buying a home in that area.

Reclaimed wood flooring and beams from an old local farmhouse add authenticity. The doors and windows came from Old World Antieks in La Grange, while the coffee table was rescued from a Los Angeles hotel by Katy's mother.

OPPOSITE: *This slender table serves a variety of purposes: paired with a garden chair, it works as a desk, a place to enjoy a snack or simply a stage on which to display favorite seasonal items.*

BELOW: *A composition of dried pods gathered from a local tree in a simple ceramic pot and an old piece of driftwood inscribed with a peaceful sentiment confer an organic feel.*

RIGHT: *The old credenza/sideboard from Bill Moore Antiques in Carmine appealed to Katy not only for its weathered finish and compact size but also for its capacity to conceal items dedicated to laid-back indoor pursuits. The sign was a "lucky" find.*

"Right before I retired, we started looking for a place to flip, fix or rent," Katy says. When they couldn't find what they had in mind, the pair decided to build on a small lot they owned in town. They were intrigued by the trend of using old grain silos, either alone or blended with new construction. "My friend and contractor Judy Kurtz had built a few silo cabins," Katy says. "They were so cute and different, but we needed something a bit bigger with more amenities so that it could be rented out when we weren't using it ourselves." Instead, the Halligans proposed to attach a silo to the small home they wanted to build together. "Will and I drew a sketch on a piece of paper and Judy ran with the idea," Katy recalls.

ABOVE: *Open shelves give the kitchen an airy look. A shutter from The Vintage Rose Market in Fayetteville conceals the pantry and, with the custom stove/cooker hood, imbues the space with rustic charm.*

The couple bought a 300-square-foot/28-square-meter silo from a nearby farm. Once their new 600-square-foot/56-square-meter house was complete, with a design inspired by their small cottage in Northern California, it was time to unite both structures.

"We tried to include as many conveniences as we could, since it would not only be a getaway for us but also used for short-term rentals," Katy explains. In fact, the cottage, which they named The Rusty Clover, has become one of the region's favorite Airbnb listings.

LEFT: *A spiral staircase leads to a small loft with twin beds to accommodate guests. A diminutive butcher block fits perfectly between the stairs and the found door to the bathroom.*

ABOVE: *Though it looks old, the vanity was custom-built for the small bathroom and fitted with new fixtures in keeping with the homespun style. Baskets, a shelf and a peg rack offer storage with style.*

ABOVE LEFT: *Old shutters stand at the entrance to the bedroom located in the converted silo. The laundry area and walk-in closets are concealed on either side of the hallway.*

ABOVE RIGHT: *A cabinet found with missing drawers turned out to be perfect for Katy to stash storage baskets. An old post turned into a coat rack keeps jackets and shirts within reach.*

OPPOSITE: *The 300-square-foot/28-square-meter silo bedroom is Katy's favorite room. "The ceiling itself is a work of art, and the glow from the stained-glass window is beautiful," she says.*

I love looking around and remembering where everything came from.

Storage is a big component of making a small home function at its best. "We made a lot of changes to our original plan as we went along. For example, we had intended to put the washer and dryer in the bathroom, but that would have made the space too tight. Instead, we expanded the hallway that links the silo to the house to accommodate a separate laundry area and a large walk-in closet," Katy explains.

Although Will was instrumental in the initial planning and building, when it came to decorating, Katy had free rein. "I was in my element," she says with a smile. "Our other homes have a lot of stuff"—a condition she calls "antiques dealer's disease"—"but here, my focus was clean, easy and cozy."

TAKE A CHANCE
Bring energy to a subdued palette with well-chosen pops of color.

ABOVE: *Once used to store grain, the little silo has been given a new purpose as an addition to the small cottage Katy and Will built on their land.*

RIGHT: *Furnished with comfort and relaxation in mind, the screened-in back porch serves up local charm and plenty of room for friendly gatherings or for quietly watching nature unfold.*

However, she does admit she started buying for the house a bit too early. "After all, we are so close to Round Top! I got a lot of the furnishings from dealer friends. I love looking around and remembering who and where everything came from. I did end up with a few pieces that didn't work out for us, but it was easy to sell them on because I had a little spot in one of the shops in town."

Katy says she doesn't have a specific style in mind when undertaking a decorating project. "I always start with one key piece, and then work from there and just go with things I love. Somehow it all fits together, with, of course, a little trial and error along the way!" The result is a comfy, one-of-a-kind compact hideaway with rooms that take on a collected approach. Each piece has a distinct purpose and significance, adding up to a whole that honors its local roots.

Despite its period details and historic value, this
19th-century cottage was slated for the wrecking ball
until a couple on the hunt for a small home stepped in.

PAST PERFECT

*OPPOSITE: Dna designed and built the pine
benches and table to make the most of
the narrow breakfast room. Half
curtains allow the natural light in while
providing privacy.*

*ABOVE: The couple brought the once-
dilapidated cottage back to its intricate
Victorian-era architecture. The new
front porch was designed by Dna with
respect to the home's roots.*

Joan Jusell, a former kindergarten teacher, and her
husband Dna Hoover, a contractor, were looking to
move from their spacious home in Vacaville, California
to a smaller one in the same town. "We simply weren't
using all of it and it was a lot to care for," Joan
explains. "We wanted to be in a place where we could
utilize and enjoy every room." As fate would have it,
they came across a small cottage whose owner had
decided to tear it down and build a three-unit
apartment building in its place.

"We have always been attracted to fixer-uppers and
rickety old houses, and the location was so convenient
with many amenities close by and downtown only
a few steps away," says Joan. She and Dna came up
with a plan to save the home from demolition and
also create something compatible with the original
structure and the neighborhood.

For Dna, there were many benefits to preserving
the cottage. "Saving old buildings is vital not only
to preserve the architectural continuum but also to
sequester the embodied carbon stored within," he
explains. "A well-designed, well-built and well-
maintained structure can last many hundreds of years.
It's important to try to do it right."

DIRECT TRAFFIC

Place furniture strategically to ensure ease of movement.

THIS PAGE AND OPPOSITE: *Light wood tones and unique textures come together in a cohesive palette. This creates a warm and harmonious whole and amps up the visual and comfort appeal of the room.*

DIVIDE AND CONQUER

Utilize easily movable room dividers to create intimate zones for distinct purposes within one space.

Dna and Joan chose smooth, honey-hued maple cladding for the walls, trim and ceiling, which Dna built himself. Joan wanted the rooms to have a warm, cozy and calm aesthetic with plenty of simple but interesting details.

To that end, the pair, undertook major structural and cosmetic improvements, including gutting and rebuilding the core of the home. 'We reused as many materials as possible," Joan says. "We were moving along with the project, but we had to stop when Dna fell off the porch roof and broke his back. However, we were fortunate to have contractors and friends come to the rescue and help secure the home before the winter weather arrived." Once he had recovered, Dna was able to resume working on the interior. He increased the total footprint to 1,100 square feet/102 square meters with an addition that now accommodates a galley-style kitchen. He also installed stylish honey-hued maple wood walls, trims, ceilings and built-in joinery in the living room and breakfast room, where they confer a modern aesthetic.

Next it was Joan's turn to take the lead on decorating the interiors. "I used to have many collections, but moving to this cottage made me rethink my style," she says. "What appealed to me was the notion of both small-space living and conscious consumption." Though streamlined, the home has a warm and welcoming mood. Its monochromatic palette is enhanced by leather and wood furnishings in similar tones, which add richness and texture and create the illusion of a larger space. "The most challenging area was the living room because of its size, its high ceiling and openness to the kitchen and breakfast nook. The goal was to create separate areas using movable dividers instead of walls," Joan says. "This is my favorite room because of the morning light, and also for its warm, cozy and cocoon-like ambiance."

Moving to this cottage made me rethink my style.

OPPOSITE: *To maintain the cohesive look and feel of the living space, Dna made a pine top to dress up the metal base of the dining-room table.*

RIGHT: *Easy to move and store, a child-size pine table and chairs come in handy for meals or playtime when Joan's granddaughter comes to visit with her little friends.*

FAR RIGHT: *Space and location dictated the size and shape of the new galley-style kitchen addition, which Dna built and then fitted with bespoke cabinetry, shelves and countertops. The space-saving refrigerator was a splurge.*

The couple moved in eight years ago and Joan has been slowly finding the right pieces to create the look she envisioned without adding clutter. This has involved shopping at flea markets and antiques fairs as well as at mainstream stores. "Live in your home for a while to determine what you really need," she advises. "Take your time to acquire pieces, buy only what you love and keep it simple."

Dna and Joan's dedication to rehabilitate the once-decaying home shows what can happen when you care for old buildings. Today, their cottage is timeless. The exterior shows off its architectural origins with features typical of the 1890s Eastlake style, such as porch posts and railings with intricate wooden designs and curved brackets. However, the uniquely personal interior strikes the right balance between old and new and represents the ideal blend of style and function.

OPPOSITE LEFT: *Despite being modernized, the bathroom retains its original flavor with a handmade frosted glass door and redwood cabinet. A found vintage basin with a raised shelf lends convenient storage space.*

OPPOSITE RIGHT AND THIS PAGE: *In the master bedroom, a wall-to-wall closet opposite the bed belies the usual expectations of storage particular to small homes. Though not in use, the Dutch door was kept for its vintage appeal and value.*

When Ki Nassauer's daughter and son-in-law invited her to come and live in the guesthouse of their newly purchased home, the timing couldn't have been more serendipitous.

LIVED-IN STYLE

"It was during the pandemic, and I was thrilled to 'bubble' with them and my grandchildren," Ki says. Though she had been used to living in much larger homes than the 660-square-foot/61-square-meter guest cottage, the opportunity of being close to her grandkids far outweighed the challenges of downsizing from a spacious three-bedroom apartment. "My homes have fluctuated in size ever since I moved to Los Angeles more than 10 years ago. All had benefits that were not necessarily dictated by size: a porch, a quiet neighborhood, a crafting room with storage, interesting architectural details and other varied perks. But none could have competed with the obvious advantage attached to this little place," Ki says.

Her living quarters' new and perfect condition was another bonus. "That was a first for me," says Ki, who had spent her life painting, patching, fixing and remodeling all the homes she had ever lived in. "I never knew what move-in ready meant!" Ki has crafted a career from scouring antiques shops, flea markets, salvage yards and the occasional street-side pile of castoffs for materials to create inventive furniture and accessories for

ABOVE: *The open-plan space incorporates living and dining areas and a streamlined kitchen. Ki had to let go of two favorite leather chairs to accommodate the sofa so that she can snuggle up with her grandchildren. The pillows/cushions are from Ikea and Etsy.*

national magazines. The one big drawback of downsizing was having to part with many favorite pieces that she had collected over time. "I sold or donated what I absolutely didn't love (and have few regrets), fashioned storage racks outside using plastic tubs, fireplace log holders and waterproof covers, and utilized under-the-bed storage bins for my stash of vintage trinkets that I just couldn't get rid of."

ABOVE: *The top of the bookcase is one of the few surfaces that lends itself to showing off rotating displays of books and one-of-a-kind items. Ki uses this whimsical carved wooden bird to hold cards, photos or outgoing mail.*

CURATED DISPLAYS

Keep handy the things you use every day and keep visible the things you love. Rotate accessories in and out of storage seasonally if you would like to display more of your favorites.

ABOVE: *The metal carousel horse, a prized possession, stands ready for action by a credenza/sideboard. The latter was rehabilitated by Ki, who says: "It has become a great storage piece."*

RIGHT: *The key to Ki's cheerful living area is clean-lined furniture with crisp, textural fabrics and simple silhouettes. The space is enlivened by rainbow-hued accessories and nostalgic details such as the iconic city posters and a 1960s-style pedestal table from Room & Board.*

GO HIGH

Tall shelving units and cabinets are ideal for small spaces—just make sure you keep a stepladder handy.

LEFT: *A custom iron stand turns a metal egg transport box into a unique side table. The vase is an example of Nemadji pottery from Minnesota.*

RIGHT: *In the bedroom, past and current furnishings unite to establish a sense of harmony. A reclaimed metal cabinet has been reincarnated as a nightstand/ bedside table, while the tall wooden locker holds linens, toiletries and cleaning supplies. The artwork above the bed is from Fine Art America..*

Letting go was a difficult process, but it gave Ki the opportunity to create a cohesive, uncluttered interior and allow some of her remaining favorite art and vintage items a spot to shine, though as she explains, "Wall space was super tricky, since my walls have either windows, doors or cabinets." Looking around the rooms, it is clear that Ki had a plan right from the beginning. "I imagined a colorful and eclectic space where my grandchildren would be free to craft, play and cozy up. A space where I could continue to work while enjoying my personal treasures in a curated environment. A space that oozed a lived-in style."

Ki says that her love of the authentic and the unique began early on. "My mom had a more modern, minimalist style. Growing up, I learned to appreciate the restful moments she created in our homes. Too much stuff makes me anxious. I am most comfortable in a 'less is more' environment." Among her most-loved possessions, Ki cites her black-and-white spotted vintage metal carousel horse, which was a birthday present from her family. "After I mentioned that I had fallen in love with it at a flea market but didn't feel I could spend the money on such an expensive personal item, they gifted me with that beauty," she recalls.

I am most comfortable in a "less is more" environment.

ABOVE LEFT: *A neutral backdrop and fittings keep the bathroom up to date. The three-dimensional geometric pattern of the floor tiles adds a graphic punch, while the gray wall tiles in the shower draw the eye upward. The overall effect is chic yet modern.*

ABOVE RIGHT: *Even the bathroom doesn't escape Ki's fondness for time-honored touches. A tarnished silver cup becomes a vase in which to display vibrant blooms and a vintage dish makes room for lotion and other small sundries.*

OPPOSITE: *A framed photograph by David Parise of vintage Barbie® and Ken® dolls in a beach setting inspires a trip down memory lane. The industrial stool makes a fitting spot for a stack of whimsical, colorful polka-dot towels from Anthropologie.*

When asked about her favorite storage piece, she quickly answers: "Hands down, the spectacular Brunswick wooden bowling locker. When you run across a 'never before seen' vintage item at a flea market, you know you need to snag it quickly." She also describes the locker as her biggest indulgence. "I never regretted the purchase, even though it was more than I would typically spend on one cabinet. It is the best storage unit I could wish for!"

For over a decade, as editor of *Flea Market Style* magazine, Ki connected a national network of vintage and antiques aficionados and devoted fans. They have embraced her unique style, which is now the subject of her *Lived-In Style* magazine and her recently released book of the same name, which is aptly subtitled "the art of creating a feel-good home". In both, she shares her passion for the beauty and utility of a vintaged-inspired lifestyle.

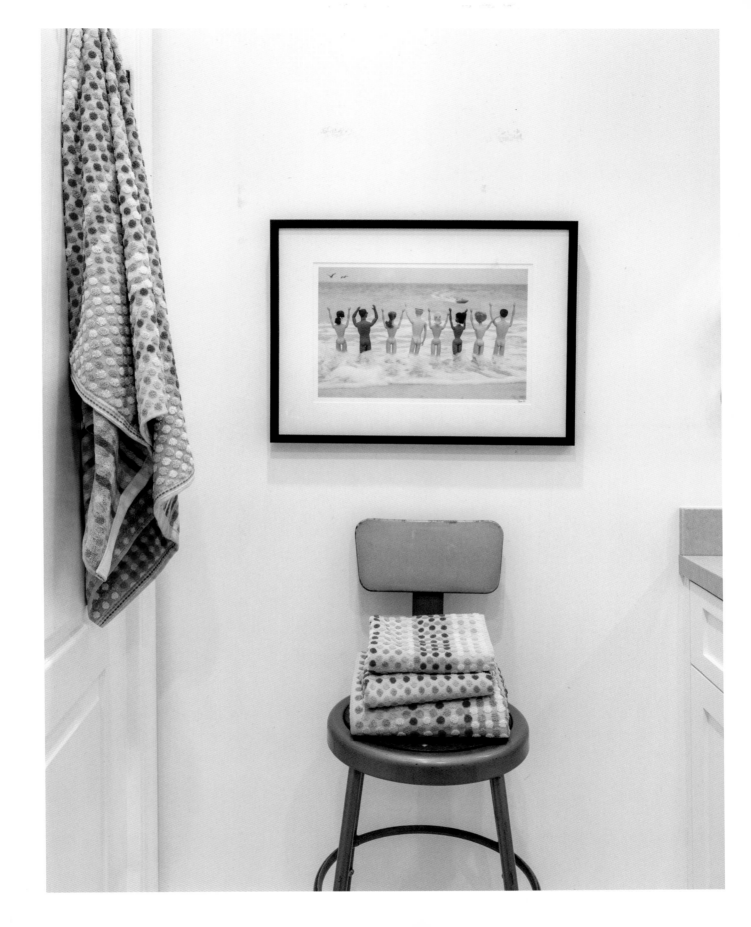

After years of living in apartments, Jenna Kinghorn and her husband Iain set out to find a home of their own and discovered the perfect bungalow in the town of Riverside, Rhode Island.

TRUE BLUE

OPPOSITE: *Jenna painted the porch floor, table and rocking chair in her favorite blue hues. The vintage pillows/cushions continue the classic color palette.*

ABOVE LEFT: *The shelving unit, a family heirloom, was refinished by Jenna, who also painted the wooden sign by hand.*

ABOVE RIGHT: *The thrifted bed, from Acushnet River Antiques in New Bedford, Massachusetts, is Jenna's proudest DIY project. She cut it down to size, sealed the original chippy paintwork and made it a new mattress.*

The 1,000-square-foot/93-square-meter property is situated on a picket-fenced corner lot in a quiet neighborhood of the former resort town, which dates back to the late 1800s. Its storybook qualities caught the couple's eye.

"It was just the right size for us and our four kitties Teddy, Agnes, Remy and Charlotte," Jenna recalls. "The moment we walked in, we fell in love with the flow of the rooms and the architectural features: the arched doorways, wood floors and moldings and beadboard ceiling in the porch."

Luckily, the home was in great condition. The only space in need of a major refit was the bathroom, which had a pink-and-brown 1960s vibe. "We gutted it and renovated the entire room, installing a new shower, toilet, sink and flooring," says Jenna, who is a self-taught interior decorator.

"Everything else has been cosmetic. I've worked room by room, painting and wallpapering in my signature shades of blue and white." Jenna's interiors style is heavily influenced by her travels, whether in the English countryside, Iain's native Scotland or northern France, where the couple has a vacation home. Her favorite colors are a classic pairing that never dates and is dependably fresh. "I've always loved how calming and cozy blue and white feel," she says. "It's also my husband's favorite combination, as they're the colors of the Scottish flag." Jenna's signature palette even inspired the name of her online shop, Blanc & Bleu, which offers a curated collection of vintage finds, handmade goods and upcycled furniture.

Although decorating comes naturally to Jenna, she says her biggest challenge was figuring out the layout and the placement of her furniture. "Smaller rooms require being creative with not only how you arrange furnishings but also what you will actually use in that space," she notes.

LEFT: *In the cozy living room, blue accents rest against a white backdrop. A narrow coffee table and slender credenza/ sideboard balance the ample sofa.*

ABOVE: *With its picket fence, vine-draped arbor and blooming shrubs, the little 1928 cottage offers plenty of curb appeal.*

CREATIVE STORAGE

Keep clutter at bay by putting vintage and new baskets, crocks and other containers to work storing miscellaneous items.

ABOVE LEFT: *A vertical shelving unit doesn't take up much space and lends itself to an array of storage choices, including baskets, boxes and other attractive containers. It can also be used for original seasonal displays.*

ABOVE RIGHT TOP AND BOTTOM: *The fireplace surround gets a makeover with peel-and-stick wallpaper that resembles old French tiles. A vintage champagne bucket used as a vase holds stems of blue thistles, mixing beauty with practicality.*

OPPOSITE: *As is often the case in older homes, the kitchen, dining and living rooms are open to one another. In the dining area, a round table and a circular rug help facilitate foot traffic.*

MULTITASKING

Whenever possible, incorporate pieces that can perform more than one function. A dresser/chest of drawers doubles as a work surface, while the drawers and cabinets offer ample storage for all types of items.

Maison
Boudonnais
BOULANGERIE · PATISSERIE
36   36

OPPOSITE AND THIS PAGE: *The back entrance offers a multi-functional space that serves as a mud room and as an extension to the kitchen. Jenna takes full advantage of the storage possibilities with hooks, baskets of all sizes and shapes, wall shelves and a versatile dresser/chest of drawers.*

OPPOSITE: *Jenna loves to cook, so the Ilve stove/cooker was a must for its high performance and timeless design. Copper pots (from her online store Blanc & Bleu) and whitewashed bricks emphasize the kitchen's cottage style.*

RIGHT: *Cabinetry painted white sets the tone of the galley-style kitchen. Blue-and-white dishes displayed on the upper level keep the color scheme front and center.*

BELOW: *A staple of the French country kitchen, a freestanding cupboard plays garde-manger for fresh produce while keeping everyday dishes handy.*

"My original plan for the living room changed once I remeasured it before we moved in. I ended up having to get rid of several pieces that just didn't work for the space." Her advice? Map out the floor plan and measure, measure, measure! Avoiding clutter is also high on her list of priorities. "When it comes to buying furniture or accessories, I have a rule that nothing new comes in unless something old goes out."

True to herself, Jenna keeps an open mind and is well prepared when it comes to shopping. She will scour thrift stores as well as flea markets and major retailers to find just the right items. "I always carry a notebook full of color samples, fabric swatches and measurements for each room, as well as a wish list of items we need, which I can refer to if I come across something that might work," she explains.

Compromise is essential for making a small home comfortable.

"We wanted a home that would be both pretty and practical. Everything needed to be functional, useful and comfortable but also to fit my vision of a cottage-style interior. I sourced a mix of new and vintage pieces, many of which I personally made over with paint or upholstery."

Jenna's organizational skills and fondness for classic French rural style are apparent in these carefully edited and lovingly appointed rooms, which she has allowed to breathe and flow. "It comes down to being aware of your space and sticking with only what you feel is necessary—compromise is essential for making a small home comfortable," she says.

She has some simple advice for anyone embarking on a similar project. "Live in your home for a good six months before changing anything. This will give you an idea of what works, what doesn't and what changes need to happen. Make the smart investment by doing things once and right. Don't do temporary fixes, which end up costing more in the end."

ABOVE: *The small bathroom, which previously looked rather dated, underwent a total remodel. It now has all new fixtures and cottage-style beadboard and tiles. Jenna painted the little shelves for additional storage.*

RIGHT: *Jenna upholstered the headboard of this thrifted bed in a favorite blue fabric. She then added a vintage quilt, a French pillow and a patterned wallpaper from Serena & Lily. A chair acts as a nightstand/bedside table. The framed photographs were taken by Angie Wendricks of County Road Living.*

Elyse Major has long had a love affair with little houses. So it's no wonder that when the time came to buy one, she knew exactly what to look for: a cozy home with character, more specifically a Cape Cod-style cottage in a small town.

VINTAGE VIBES

"My husband Jeff and I were drawn to Smithfield, Rhode Island for its high-ranking public school system and its affordability, which don't always go together," Elyse recalls. "We knew the area from visiting its orchards for apple picking with our boys Jonah and Ethan when they were small. Once we had decided on the town, we just needed to find the cottage!"

It didn't take long for the couple to zero in on a 1,100-square-foot/102-square-meter home with the classic New England style they coveted. "Typically, Cape Cod-style homes have many small rooms, which I knew could morph over time—a playroom becomes a study becomes a bedroom, offering versatility," Elyse explains. "I also love the architectural details such as the arched doorways, hardwood floors and shiplap ceiling in the upstairs master bedroom."

The 1949 home had seen a few improvements over the years, but was in need of a new roof and front steps. "Other than that, most everything we did has been cosmetic and very much on a shoestring," says Elyse. "The timing was perfect, as I was discovering home-decorating magazines and DIY TV shows.

THIS PAGE: *The armoire/wardrobe was one of the first pieces Elyse and Jeff bought for the house for its versatile storage possibilities. It holds everything from dishware to dish towels/tea towels and small appliances.*

OPPOSITE: *A tall but slender Pottery Barn etagere, painted white to blend in with the walls, provides space-saving vertical storage for everyday items.*

I felt inspired to try my hand at a range of projects throughout the home. I painted walls and upcycled furniture—my tinkering activities went into overdrive." Elyse's love of "tinkering" even led her to author two books on the subject: *Tinkered Treasures* and *Seaside Tinkered Treasures*.

Elyse has long been smitten with little beach cottages and that ideal is always part of her decorating ethos. Not only does she favor a seaside palette, she also loves to use foraged pebbles, sea glass and shells as accents, without losing sight of what makes a practical home. "My current version of cottage style is very much influenced by two UK designers: Atlanta Bartlett, who mixes worn furnishings with elements like shiny disco balls, and Christina Strutt of the iconic Cabbages & Roses. These creative and resourceful women have always brought an approachability to their designs and are known for working with what they have—it goes from being aspirational to inspirational."

GET CREATIVE
Use peg racks, hooks and furnishings with hidden storage wherever you can.

ABOVE LEFT: *Tucked into a corner, a bookcase-turned-pantry offers additional storage to keep canned goods, spices and other kitchen staples within reach.*

ABOVE RIGHT AND OPPOSITE: *Elyse has reimagined the entrance to the kitchen to make it a fun and useful space. She added a peg rack, from which she hangs fabric shopping bags, mugs and jars of utensils. The wallpaper was designed by Danika Herrick for Spoonflower.*

Keeping spaces flowing, establishing a system for organization and creating sufficient storage are often the biggest challenges faced by owners of small homes. "Even without an open floor plan, it's likely that most rooms on the main level are in view, so adhering to a single-color palette or thematic vibe throughout will create a cohesive feel," Elyse says.

She also has advice for keeping clutter at bay. "Through the years I've learned that furniture needs to have storage. I joke that if someone leaves a backpack or sneakers in the living room, it's an instant mess—or the remains of a wild party! Small rooms don't have the space to absorb random stuff. I'm also a big proponent of hooks. My boys can say this in unison with me: hooks turn any spot into usable space."

LEFT AND ABOVE: *A large bookcase and a credenza/sideboard offer much-needed storage in the living room, with curtains to conceal their contents. Beach finds, including shells and starfish, are displayed on the coffee table.*

Walls are put to work with mirrors to enlarge the space, ledges to display family photos and a peg rack to hang favorite notes and cards. A ladder offers additional storage for throws and blankets.

CREATE FLOW

Maximize visual space by painting both walls and ceilings the same light colors.

ABOVE: *By positioning an armoire/ wardrobe on one side of a small, recessed corner of the bedroom and furnishing the space minimally, Elyse created a snug home office area.*

RIGHT: *To take advantage of floor space, the bed is set under the lowest part of the ceiling. Floral pillows from Cabbages & Roses and a patchwork quilt add cheerful color and pattern. The narrow Ikea bench is handy for storage in spite of its compact size.*

BELOW: *Elyse's fondness for small spaces extends to dollhouses, which she builds herself. She makes their furnishings to scale so that she can experiment with layouts and styling in miniature.*

RIGHT: *The craft room, affectionately dubbed "the girlie office," is where Elyse dreams up her numerous creative projects. These became the basis for her two Tinkered Treasures books on DIY and home decor.*

As editor-in-chief at Providence Media, Elyse oversees four monthly magazines. With her busy career and two sons in college to support, time and money for decorating projects are rather more difficult to come by these days. However, whenever possible, Elyse still loves to visit and support small shops in and around Smithfield, which provide her with ample inspiration for her cottage. "There are so many wonderful makers and sellers local to us. It's an opportunity to decorate with pieces that are unique to Rhode Island."

With its clever use of space, personality and nostalgic vibe, Elyse's home mirrors her ingenuity, creativity and winning make-do attitude.

USE NATURE'S GIFT
Keep window treatments minimal to allow in as much natural light as possible.

MODERN EASE

From its original use as a laboratory through several reincarnations, this turn-of-the-century building in California has had many lives and has finally found its *raison d'être* as a home with singular beauty.

CONCEAL AND REVEAL

Showcase your favorite pieces, but keep the number in each display to a minimum for more impact and to avoid clutter.

OPPOSITE: Furnishings with sleek finishes and low profiles, including a Jøtul cast-iron stove, coax the interior into the here and now, with plenty of room to breathe and pared-back beauty.

ABOVE LEFT: Thoughtfully selected accessories, such as this miniature wooden canoe, are valued for their organic and handcrafted qualities.

ABOVE RIGHT: A curvy ceramic vase, handmade by Noah's mother, can be moved around to wherever it is needed, but is always given pride of place.

Built in 1907, the 1,100-square-foot/102-square-meter building is home to the visionary designer Noah Guy and his partner, photographer Aysia Stieb. It was clear to Noah that a lot of work and time had been invested in the property over the years, but equally evident was the need to undo some of the less sympathetic alterations. "It doesn't fit a specific architectural style, as it was built as a chemist's laboratory out of poured concrete," he explains. "Because of this, the building does to this day have a striking originality and quality. Though it was never intended to be a residence, clearly various people had inhabited it for several decades and along the way many changes were made that were at odds with the stunning austerity of the original structure."

In addition to its unquestionably unique history, construction and design, the building has an attractive location in Berkeley, Northern California—high up on a hill with a large retaining wall and a private garden—which only added to Noah's belief in its potential.

MAKE IT CLEAR

The right lighting makes all
the difference in helping
a small place look larger
than its actual size.

LEFT: *A curated mix of contemporary furnishings, handmade pieces and artifacts informs Noah's reductionist approach to design while enhancing the home's architecture and the aged patina of the concrete walls. Pieces with durable textures combine function and essential creature comforts. Next to an iconic Le Corbusier chaise longue from Design Within Reach, Goa the dog enjoys a leather pillow/cushion from Noah's own brand Joshuvela.*

ABOVE: *A library corner is established with floor-to-ceiling shelves from Rakks, a tall and slender lamp, a graphic table and a metal-framed leather chair.*

"My goal was to pay respect to the original builder's and architect's work by eradicating all the previous poor attempts to make the building into a residence and rolling back to the original interior plan but with some modern updates," he says.

Time and money were the main concerns. The San Francisco Bay Area is notorious for expensive real estate and materials, so Noah undertook much of the labor by himself. "It added several years to the project, but it brought the cost down and the quality way up," he says. "The building itself was sound, but we had to update just about everything, including all the systems and the interiors. I carried out the necessary changes to make the structure more habitable—adding modern and technological improvements, but at the same time enhancing the original design."

ABOVE LEFT: *In the new kitchen, wall-to-wall cabinets coated with recycled plastic lend high style and generous storage options and space-saving recesses for appliances.*

ABOVE RIGHT: *Noah custom-built the island using raw steel, blackened and coated with beeswax, for the base and lower shelf. The top is a reclaimed maple butcher block from his former home.*

RIGHT: *Noah often uses the dining area as a space where he can work on his designs. The table he built offers an ample surface for drawing, laying out plans and photographing finished items. Classic mid-century modern dining chairs designed by Hans J. Wegner and Charles and Ray Eames are teamed with simple seats from Ikea.*

Though each room serves a specific function, a consistent palette of colors and textures seamlessly brings together the living and dining areas with the entry and kitchen, illustrating the transformative power of design. Used for household storage, a record player and USM metal cabinets subtly delineate the transition from the living room to the dining space.

Natural materials create a more organic and calming experience.

STORAGE SAVVY

When using containers to corral items, stick with identical ones for a unified look.

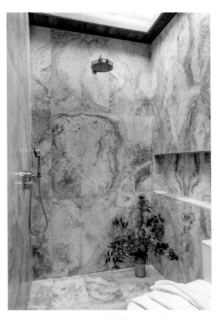

OPPOSITE: *Noah built this shelving unit and made leather baskets to fit, combining practicality with exquisite design.*

ABOVE LEFT: *White walls, warm wood, sparse furnishings and natural light bring a sense of space to the bedroom. Houseplants add to the serene mood.*

ABOVE RIGHT TOP AND BOTTOM: *With its travertine-clad walls and floors, the bathroom appears to have been chiseled out of solid stone. The spun stainless steel Japanese sink highlights the quiet eloquence of the design.*

Noah names modern architecture and interiors, simple and honest materials and ancient building techniques as major influences on his personal decorating style, which he defines as "reductionist." "I like that when using real materials throughout the building, you can create a more beautiful lived-in experience," he explains. "Natural materials such as steel, wood and stone create a more organic and calming experience."

It took a long time, but Noah and Aysia have succeeded in transforming this structure into an exceptional home. The space welcomes with its inspired redesign based on inviting, comfortable simplicity, while still celebrating its industrial-minimalist origins.

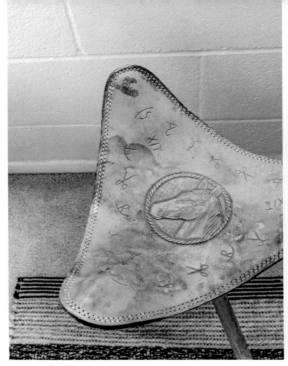

There is something about houses that never fails to ignite interior stylist and photographer Sunday Hendrickson's creativity, even when it came to reinventing a once-nondescript cottage into an enchanting home.

LITTLE OASIS

OPPOSITE: *Cleverly positioned at an angle, a comfortable chair nestles in the corner of the living room without blocking the entrance to the kitchen.*

ABOVE LEFT: *A versatile and portable vintage leather stool can easily be stored away or brought out to provide extra seating whenever the need arises.*

ABOVE RIGHT: *When topped with a tray, the same little stool takes on a new function by morphing into a convenient side table.*

Getting homes photo-ready for 30 years has made Sunday the darling of countless magazines, architects and advertising agencies. (Two homes she styled and photographed for this book are featured on pages 20–31 and 32–43.) But after decades living in Los Angeles, the time had come for a move to a quieter area while keeping within reach of the city for her work. So two years ago, Sunday gave up the big-city lifestyle for the bucolic landscape, small-town quaintness and laid-back charm of Ojai, California.

Downsizing applied not only to her choice of physical location but to her home as well, which came naturally to her. "Growing up, I shared a bedroom with my two sisters and we had one bathroom for our family of five, so I was well trained," she recalls. "My next home was an apartment in New York City, and then I lived in apartments and a home in Los Angeles. By the time I moved here, it was a piece of cake."

LAYER, LAYER, LAYER
For the coziest feel without adding bulk, include soft throws, fluffy pillows/cushions and inviting area rugs.

ABOVE: *To maximize the potential of an unused corner, Sunday hung a one-of-a-kind peg rack, fashioned from antlers, to stand in as a catch-all place to keep her walking stick and other outdoor gear.*

RIGHT: *Despite its size, the living room is big on comfort. The sofa opens into a bed for overnight guests. Vintage suitcases and a sideboard with sliding doors afford storage for personal items as well as linens and other home goods.*

AMERICAN PORTRAIT

Eden Grinshpan   EATING OUT LOUD

LIFE   FRANS LANTING

ABOVE: *It is all in the details. Little ceramic placecard holders in the shape of piglets are both useful and decorative. Soft green accents keep the setting light and airy.*

OPPOSITE: *The built-in bookcase acts as a divider between both rooms but allows a partial view of the kitchen through its open shelves. This creates a visual flow and ensures a seamless transition between the two spaces.*

ABOVE: *When not needed for small gatherings, the table in the eating area is placed flush with the wall to facilitate foot traffic in the kitchen. The slender design of the Laclasica chairs by Stua, from Design Within Reach, further contributes to the efficient use of space.*

Her diminutive newfound nest was bright and airy, despite its 400-square-foot/37-square-meter footprint. However, the 1950s cinder-block construction presented something of a challenge. "I had never lived in that type of space before, but I decided to embrace the industrial vibe and it worked out," she says. "It was clean and had a new coat of gray paint with white trim—it only needed some cosmetic improvements." The first thing on her list was getting rid of the kitchen's original "hospital-green" backsplash and countertops. Covering the former with a black pin-striped canvas and painting the latter a glossy white disguised their dated appearance and gave the space a new energy with a hint of drama.

"Furnishing the cottage was another issue," Sunday explains. "I had to let go of most of what I owned, but it was cathartic. Luckily, I have a friend who owns a vintage shop, so she came over and took everything: pictures on the walls, rugs, lamps, chairs, curtains, you name it. That was the deal— she had to take it all, deduct her commission and give the rest to charity.

It worked out perfectly and saved moving fees!" Sunday was ready for a new look and she was willing to start again from scratch in order to decorate her new home. Fortunately, she had moved to the right place.

One of the many charms of Ojai is that it doesn't feature any chain stores. Instead, it boasts small, one-of-a-kind shops that sell the unique and artistic wares favored by the residents of the little town. "The many years I had spent arranging and styling other people's homes for my job taught me what works and what doesn't," Sunday says. Her aim was to create comfortable and friendly spaces, which she accomplished with

BE SIZE WISE

Getting the scale right is essential in a small space, so take the dimensions of each room into account.

OPPOSITE: *With space and storage critical, Sunday opted to go vertical. A cabinet from Tumbleweed & Dandelion and sets of labeled drawers sit atop her custom-made desk. An industrial metal rack holds files and documents.*

ABOVE: *The queen-size bed fits snugly in the corner. With so little floor space to spare, a pendant light is both functional and stylish. A vintage trunk at the foot of the bed keeps spare throws and pillows/cushions easily accessible.*

mostly upholstered furniture with no sharp edges or fussiness. The combination of a soft, neutral palette, touchable texture and timeless pieces has established a soothing atmosphere.

Due to the compact size of her home, another of Sunday's goals was to make sure every item had a clearly defined purpose, often several. For instance, the living-room sofa doubles up as a bed for guests, the end table nearby also provides space for books and magazines and the stack of vintage suitcases, which might seem primarily decorative, keeps wrapping paper, ribbons and other sundries organized and out of sight.

FAR LEFT: *A table with a drawer affords additional storage to the vanity. Besides its usual function, the mirror visually expands the room.*

LEFT ABOVE: *First-aid supplies and bathroom sundries are neatly and safely stowed in labeled metal boxes and shelved with bath towels and other everyday necessities.*

LEFT BELOW: *Glass jars make it easy to see their contents at a glance while safeguarding them from little hands.*

OPPOSITE: *Comfortable, minimal furnishings in the same materials and finishes and a profusion of potted plants transform a barren spot into a private oasis for relaxation and entertaining.*

I am right in the heart of my little town.

"When decorating a small place, it's important to keep things simple, minimal and functional, and work with tones and textures rather than a variety of colors." Sunday advises. "And don't buy anything unless you have absolutely fallen in love with it!"

When asked if she feels moving to Ojai was the right decision, Sunday is quick to answer: "My home is part of an enclave of four little cottages, so there is that small-town camaraderie. We look after each other and each other's pets! Also, I am right in the heart of my little town, and I can walk everywhere without having to experience the Los Angeles traffic. Days go by when I don't have to get in the car—I can even walk to a dozen different hiking trails. This little place and its pastoral surroundings are everything I was hoping for and all I need."

BE SELECTIVE

Think "a place for everything and everything in its place." Pare down to the essentials and the things you truly love.

If you drive through Solvang, in California's lush Santa Ynez Valley, you will fall under the spell of the small town's European charm, just as Joanne Gordon did.

CALIFORNIA CHARMER

"I love the area and the country feel of my neighborhood, where I'm surrounded by horses and donkey ranches," Joanne says. "After 35 years, I was ready to downsize from the home where I raised my two boys. When I drove by this cottage, I was instantly smitten. The front garden had a rose-draped arbor, a little picket fence and a brick path bordered with an abundance of white roses in bloom. It was dreamy!"

Not only was Joanne charmed by the home's curb appeal and location but it also answered her wish list. "I wanted a small home with a spacious outdoor entertaining space," she says. "A cozy little place that would allow me to declutter my life and live with only the things I need and that make me happy, not a home with empty rooms filled with stuff that's never used."

OPPOSITE AND ABOVE: Vintage and new furnishings come together to create a sense of simple elegance on the inviting front porch, which is surrounded by lush shrubbery, fragrant roses and flowering trees. Antique accents bring romantic farmhouse style and balance the modernity of the wicker chairs.

ABOVE: *To show off meaningful items without creating clutter, Joanne had shelves built on either side of the living-room window. This allows her to create orderly displays, which can easily be moved around and updated over time.*

RIGHT: *Jodi Goldberg of Jodi G Designs sourced a number of pieces for the living room. It is a study in softness and comfort, new and old, coastal and rustic. Blue accents, including a beaded chandelier from Regina Andrew, speak of Joanne's fondness for the ocean, while gently weathered pieces speak of her penchant for farmhouse decor.*

GET HELP

Don't shy away from hiring professional help for decorating or organizing.

At 975 square feet/91 square meters, the cottage was a perfect fit. Add a large lot for outdoor gatherings and mix in a Dutch door or two, a tin roof and a sheltered front porch and you will understand why Joanne says: "I had to have it!" The interior had also been lovingly maintained, she recalls. "The previous homeowner kept the vintage character but made it better, right down to the original wood floors with layers of white paint. They gave the cottage a very clean and bright feel."

The home was furnished with mostly French farmhouse-inspired pieces, but while Joanne opted to incorporate some of the style, she also wanted to bring in her collection of corals and sea fans for more of a coastal farmhouse vibe with a feminine twist. At this point, she decided to call in the Santa Barbara-based designer Jodi Goldberg of Jodi G Designs.

ABOVE: *A low-profile credenza/sideboard provides extra storage for the kitchen overflow of dinnerware reserved for parties rather than for everyday meals. When not in use, the TV shows a scene with colors in keeping with the decor.*

RIGHT: *"The large hutch/dresser serves as entertaining storage for wine glasses, cocktail accessories, a place to display a collection of vintage vases, which I'm still collecting, and also artwork that hasn't yet found its spot," says Joanne.*

"I cannot thank Jodi enough for helping me with that vision—she knew the items I loved and helped mix the old with the new," Joanne says. In particular, she recalls how the scheme for the living room came together from a variety of sources. "Jodi found vintage sconces to balance with new chandeliers, a beautiful vintage rug and had a modern couch built to fit the room. She also came up with a driftwood side table, which was made to look old to offset the modern credenza/sideboard and the coffee table, which I had brought from my beach house. Finally, she added a vintage mirror to pair with my sea fans. She pulled the look together."

ABOVE LEFT: *Rather than upper cabinets, open shelves add storage and display areas without making the kitchen feel closed in. The sign, crate and hanging pans evoke farmhouse style.*

ABOVE RIGHT: *The back entrance to the cottage opens into a small laundry room. Clearly labeled boxes in the built-in cabinet keep necessities perfectly organized and readily accessible.*

OPPOSITE: *Joanne had the banquette built to make the most of the space. The little nook offers plenty of seating without interfering with foot traffic and provides additional storage inside the base.*

If I buy something new, it must have more than one purpose.

OPPOSITE: *A lack of closets is typical of small homes. Joanne solves the bedroom issue with a mirrored armoire/wardrobe from Ballard Designs, which adds depth and dimension to the room.*

ABOVE: *The master bedroom takes its feminine cue from a Serena & Lily wallpaper featuring a timeless antique print of soft-hued flowers.*

The biggest challenge for Joanne was editing down her possessions to fit the limited space. "I was able to reach my goal of decluttering, but I have many items that are hard to part with. I gave away a lot and tried to only keep what I needed, but also ended up building a shed to store holiday decorations and seasonal clothes. Nowadays, if I buy something new, it must have more than one purpose. For instance, a pitcher/jug may serve lemonade, hold fresh cut flowers or become part of my decoration."

Joanne also had to learn to be very organized. "Everything has labels and everything has a place. When I have guests, they know exactly where to find something and where to put it back."

ABOVE: *The bathroom needed to conceal essential items, be pretty and functional and maintain the master bedroom's romantic tone. Joanne incorporated a narrow sideboard, a vintage wall cabinet and flowing curtains.*

ABOVE RIGHT AND RIGHT: *The guest bedroom is all about the simplicity, comfort and charm of country life. By not setting the twin beds side by side, Joanne has freed up valuable floor space. A painting by Joanne's son Trevor and a bench-turned-side table add hints of color.*

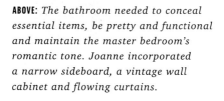

LESS IS MORE

Take an inventory of each room and keep only what's important. Purge, purge, and purge some more!

Joanne says she feels most at peace when she doesn't have clutter around her. "My closets are filled with the appropriate clothing for the season. In the summer, I pack up the winter coats and shoes and store them in the outside shed. I can't do knick-knacks, so I try to have fewer, larger items of decor. The key to living comfortably in a small space is to stay organized and have nearly every piece of furniture perform double duty. I think I have achieved that."

DRAWING BOARD

Sketch out your rooms and your current furniture to scale. Make cutouts of the items and place them on the page to figure out which pieces will work and eliminate those that won't.

LEFT: *A lack of electrical outlet options in the living room prompted the creative solution of ceiling-mounted string lights. The seating arrangement invites conversation and relaxation while highlighting the panoramic cityscape.*

RIGHT: *A view of the city, and the lake beyond, was a top priority for Jami and Katie. With its vantage point, the simply furnished balcony fulfills their wish.*

Jami Guy and Katie Bamba had three main criteria in mind when looking for a home: it had to be small, offer an easy commute to San Francisco and have a view of Lake Merritt, California.

BOHO ALLURE

"Luckily, when Katie and I began our search for the perfect place, this Oakland apartment came up for rent," Jami recalls. "It had all the features we were looking for, including two bedrooms and a balcony with an unobstructed lake view. It was also located within easy distance of work." At 1,100 square feet/102 square meters, the apartment was just the right size, too. "The condition was standard for a typical apartment: clean and functional but a bit dated."

Rentals typically come with restrictions, but some cosmetic changes were allowed, and Katie seized the opportunity. "I decided to switch out the boring black knobs and handles on the kitchen cabinets and drawers for fun gold ones that are much more suited to our style," she says.

KNOW YOUR BUDGET

Furniture is pricey, so buy secondhand whenever possible. A little bit of DIY goes a long way in making them yours.

OPPOSITE: *A small credenza/sideboard gives a formerly redundant corner a sense of purpose. Greenery and diverse containers contribute a boho flavor.*

ABOVE LEFT AND RIGHT: *To create more visual fluidity than could be achieved with solid, traditional furniture, Katie chose a metal chair with an open design and an elongated coffee table.*

"There was no backsplash on the kitchen walls when we moved in, but I found a renter-friendly removable peel-and-stick wallpaper with a light pink wave pattern to put behind the sink."

Katie and Jami's approach to decorating is a reflection of their personalities, hobbies, interests and open-minded attitude. "I didn't really have a vision in the beginning," Katie confesses. "How our apartment looks now is just a culmination of fun pieces we have found that somehow all work together. I like to call my style a mix of mid-century modern, minimal boho and coastal. I don't want my space to be flat or one-note, so I look out for pieces that are interesting, colorful and bold. I am a huge fan of thrifting and DIY projects, so most of our furniture has come from Goodwill, Craigslist or Facebook Marketplace. I customize and upcycle our pieces to make them unique."

OPPOSITE: *A long console and a large mirror turn an awkward corner into just the right spot for enhancing the natural light, displaying found and favorite objects and keeping storage baskets easily accessible.*

THIS PAGE: *In the kitchen, an industrial metal rack makes the most of a corner as a useful storage space for cookware and small appliances.*

Elements with similar shapes and materials, such as the circular bar cart and round table or the neon acrylic shelves and colorful artwork by Beverly Salas, promote a continuity of design. The dining set draws the eye upward, making the space appear larger.

BE PATIENT

Finding the right pieces and decorating doesn't happen overnight. Picture the size and shape of each item in your space before purchasing it.

ABOVE: *A metal grid offers a functional wall-mounted display for small items. Katie uses hers to put up family photos using wooden clothespins/pegs embellished with little red hearts.*

RIGHT: *Ladder-style shelving provides efficient storage for books and other collected items in a confined space without encroaching on foot traffic. Mirrors add dimension to any room.*

OPPOSITE: *For the sparely furnished but comfortable bedroom, Jami and Katie eschewed traditional nightstands/ bedside tables in favor of space-saving two-tier floating shelves. Practical and versatile, they are the epitome of elegant minimalist style.*

Katie says she gets a lot of inspiration for furniture and decor from Instagram and Pinterest, as well taking notes from interior-design magazines and small-space tips from Apartment Therapy. She also studies the trends at stores such as Anthropologie, CB2, West Elm and Urban Outfitters. These varied influences result in a warm, eclectic style that permeates every room.

With its view of the lake, the living room is the couple's favorite space. "It's where we spend much of our time together with our little rescue dog Pica, and it's the most decorated space of the apartment," says

Katie. The couple's love of the ocean and being near the water comes into play in the room's palette of strong turquoise, soft pinks and natural tones, which is reminiscent of a beach at sunset. However, getting the right arrangement of furniture, including a sectional/modular sofa and a daybed, was a challenge. "The fireplace juts out and creates these weird corners, so we had to figure out how to make that area function efficiently," she continues. "We wanted to mount our TV above the fireplace and have the couch face it, but we couldn't since we weren't allowed to drill holes."

I look out for pieces that are interesting, colorful and bold.

Instead, she and Jami decided to place the sofa and daybed opposite one another. "It ultimately worked out for the best, as we can enjoy the view of the lake from the daybed."

While the dining-room area takes on more of a boho vibe with neon-hued shelves, colorful accessories and art, the master bedroom offers a subdued palette. "Every year we spend a week at Joshua Tree National Park in the Mojave Desert, and we love the ethereal dusty pinks, ochers and tans particular to that area," Katie says. "We wanted to bring some of that spiritual feel into our home with restful colors and natural materials."

Though transforming a typical small rented apartment into a personal home is not easily accomplished, by embracing a variety of design influences Katie and Jami have created a distinct aesthetic with a big dose of fun and a youthful vibe.

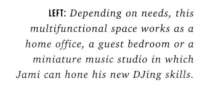

LEFT: *Depending on needs, this multifunctional space works as a home office, a guest bedroom or a miniature music studio in which Jami can hone his new DJing skills.*

ABOVE: *The spare bedroom owes its nickname, "The Mush-Room," to a tapestry Katie found, which sets the tone for fun, laid-back decor that presents variations on the theme.*

RIGHT: *Though the bathroom didn't offer many possibilities for alteration or improvement, Katie and Jami have introduced organic elements such as wooden trays and houseplants to make the space feel friendly and personal.*

SOURCES

HOMEOWNERS AND DESIGN PROFESSIONALS

Kim Kelly
www.kimkellyhomesand
design.com

Ellie Navarro
www.ellienavarro.com
www.airbnb.com/
rooms/3928797
www.vrbo.com/429019

Kristin Joyce and Don Guy
www.natuzzi.com

Katy and Will Halligan
www.airbnb.com/
rooms/704369185831593007
@therustyclover

Judy Kurtz
Bluebonnet Renovators
www.facebook.com/
bluebonnetrenovators

Ki Nassauer
www.kinassauer.com
www.livedin-style.com

Jenna and Iain Kinghorn
www.blancandbleuhome.com
@lepetitecottage

Noah Guy and Aysia Stieb
www.joshuvela.com
www.sala-studio.com

Sunday Hendrickson
www.sundayhendrickson.com

Jodi Goldberg
Jodi G Designs
www.jodigdesigns.com

US FLEA MARKETS AND ANTIQUES STORES

Acushnet River Antiques
www.acushnetriver
antiquesllc.com
New Bedford, MA

Antique Tobacco Barn
www.atbarn.com
Asheville, NC

Bill Moore Antiques
www.facebook.com/
BillMooreAntiques
Carmine, TX

Brimfield Antique Flea Markets
brimfieldantiqueflea
market.com
Brimfield, MA

Cottage Grove Vintage Market
www.cottagegrovevintage.com
Greenville, SC

Junk Bonanza
www.junkbonanza.com
Shakopee, MN

Old World Antieks
www.oldworldantieks.com
La Grange, TX

Randolph Street Market
Chicago, IL
randolphstreetmarket.com

Rose Bowl Flea Market
Pasadena, CA
rgcshows.com

Round Top Antique Shows
antiqueweekend.com
Round Top, TX

The Vintage Rose
www.vintagerosemarket.com
Fayetteville, TX

UK FLEA MARKETS AND ANTIQUES STORES

Alfies Antique Market
www.alfiesantiques.com
Marylebone, London

The Decorative Fair
www.decorativefair.com
Battersea Park, London

IACF Fairs
www.iacf.co.uk
Nationwide

Lorfords
www.lorfordsantiques.com
Tetbury, Gloucestershire

Sunbury Antiques Market
www.sunburyantiques.com
Sunbury, Surrey

FURNITURE AND HOMEWARES

Anthropologie
www.anthropologie.com
Anthropologie has scaled-down versions of some of its furniture pieces.

Apt2B
www.apt2b.com
Modern, simple and affordable furniture for apartment living.

CB2
www.cb2.com
Contemporary furniture and more.

Crate & Barrel
www.crateandbarrel.com
Crate & Barrel offers amazing options for compact spaces.

Design Within Reach
www.dwr.com
Classic mid-century modern furniture pieces.

Etsy
www.etsy.com
Handmade and vintage items from makers and sellers around the world.

HomeGoods
www.homegoods.com
Top brands at affordable prices.

Ikea
www.ikea.com
Scandi-style contemporary furniture to assemble at home.

Living Cozy
www.livingcozy.com
Recommending the best modern homeware brands.

Living Spaces
www.livingspaces.com
All kinds of furniture, including an edit for small spaces.

Pottery Barn
www.potterybarn.com
The Pottery Barn website has many photos of the brand's products in small homes.

Resource Furniture
www.resourcefurniture.com
Wall beds, extending tables and customizable cabinets.

Room & Board
www.roomandboard.com
Specially curated space-saving furniture and decor.

Serena & Lily
www.serenaandlily.com
Coastal-style furniture, wallpaper and accessories.

Tumbleweed & Dandelion
www.tumbleweed
anddandelion.com
Vintage and new pieces from interior designer Lizzie McGraw.

Urban Outfitters
www.urbanoutfitters.com
This popular brand has many items designed for apartments.

West Elm
www.westelm.com
Sustainably sourced furniture.

Williams Sonoma Home
www.williams-sonoma.com
High-end homewares.

STORAGE AND ORGANIZATION

Muji
www.muji.com
Utilitarian storage solutions.

Open Spaces
www.getopenspaces.com
Organizers and storage items.

Rakks
www.rakks.com
Architectural shelving systems.

USM
www.usm.com
Colorful modular shelves and cabinetry.

LIGHTING

Lamps Plus
www.lampsplus.com
Stylish lamps and more.

Pooky
www.pooky.com
Quirky lights from a UK brand.

Shades of Light
www.shadesoflight.com
Lighting of all kinds.

INDEX

Page numbers in *italic* refer to the illustrations.

PICTURE CREDITS

All photography by Mark Lohman unless otherwise stated.
Ph = photographer.

1 The home of Elyse and Jeff Major in Rhode Island; **2** The home of Joanne Gordon in California, designed by Jodi Goldberg of Jodi G Designs www.jodigdesigns.com; **3** The home of Ki Nassauer in California www.kinassauer.com www.lived-instyle.com; **4–5** The home of Joanne Gordon in California, designed by Jodi Goldberg of Jodi G Designs www.jodigdesigns.com; **6** Ph Sunday Hendrickson / The cottage of photographer and painter Ellie Navarro www.ellienavarro.com; **7** The home of Katy and Will Halligan in Texas @therustyclover; **8** The home of designer Kristin Joyce of Natuzzi Italia and her husband Don Guy in Florida www.natuzzi.com; **9 left** La Sala di Studio, the home of designer Noah Guy and photographer Aysia Stieb in California www.sala-studio.com; **9 right** The home of Ki Nassauer in California www.kinassauer.com www.lived-instyle.com; **10** The home of designer Kristin Joyce of Natuzzi Italia and her husband Don Guy in Florida www.natuzzi.com; **11 above left** The home of Ki Nassauer in California www.kinassauer.com www.lived-instyle.com; **11 above and below right** The home of Elyse and Jeff Major in Rhode Island; **12** The home of designer Kristin Joyce of Natuzzi Italia and her husband Don Guy in Florida www.natuzzi.com; **13 left** The home of Elyse and Jeff Major in Rhode Island; **13 right** Ph Sunday Hendrickson / The home of interior designer Kim Kelly in Georgia www.kimkellyhomesanddesign.com; **14 left** The home of interior stylist and photographer Sunday Hendrickson in California www.sundayhendrickson.com; **14 right** The home of Joanne Gordon in California, designed by Jodi Goldberg of Jodi G Designs www.jodigdesigns.com; **15** The home of Katy and Will Halligan in Texas @therustyclover; **16 above** The home of Joanne Gordon in California, designed by Jodi Goldberg of Jodi G Designs www.jodigdesigns.com; **16 below** The home of designer Kristin Joyce of Natuzzi Italia and her husband Don Guy in Florida www.natuzzi.com; **17–18** The home of stylist Jenna Kinghorn and her husband Iain in Rhode Island @lepetitecottage www.blancandbleuhome.com; **20–31** Ph Sunday Hendrickson / The home of interior designer Kim Kelly in Georgia www.kimkellyhomesanddesign.com; **32–43** Ph Sunday Hendrickson / The cottage of photographer and painter Ellie Navarro www.ellienavarro.com; **44–57** The home of designer Kristin Joyce of Natuzzi Italia and her husband Don Guy in Florida www.natuzzi.com; **58–69** The home of Katy and Will Halligan in Texas @therustyclover; **70–79** The home of Joan Jusell and her husband Dna Hoover of Dna Hoover/ Housewright in California; **80–89** The home of Ki Nassauer in California www.kinassauer.com www.lived-instyle.com; **90–101** The home of stylist Jenna Kinghorn and her husband Iain in Rhode Island @lepetitecottage www.blancandbleuhome.com; **102–113** The home of Elyse and Jeff Major in Rhode Island; **114–123** La Sala di Studio, the home of designer Noah Guy and photographer Aysia Stieb in California www.sala-studio.com; **124–133** The home of interior stylist and photographer Sunday Hendrickson in California www.sundayhendrickson.com; **134–145** The home of Joanne Gordon in California, designed by Jodi Goldberg of Jodi G Designs www.jodigdesigns.com; **146–157** The home of Jamison Guy and Katie Bamba in California.

ACKNOWLEDGMENTS

When it comes to the creation of a book, the expression "it takes a village" comes to mind. Indeed, many skilled people are involved in the process. They are the ones who make the vision come to life. It begins with the brilliant team at CICO books: publisher David Peters, senior commissioning editor Annabel Morgan, editor Sophie Devlin, creative director Leslie Harrington, art director Sally Powell, production manager Gordana Simakovic and designer Paul Tilby. Thank you for your guidance and invaluable acumen.

But let's not forget that without the gracious homeowners who welcomed us and allowed to disrupt their lives this project couldn't have happen. Heartfelt thanks to: Elyse and Jeff Major, Jenna and Iain Kinghorn, Ellie Navarro, Kim Kelly, Kristin Joyce and Don Guy, Katy and Will Halligan, Joan Jusell and Dna Hoover, Noah Guy and Aysia Stieb, Jamison Guy and Katie Bamba, Ki Nassauer, Sunday and Peachie Hendrickson, Joanne and Tilly Gordon, and a special thank you to designer Jodi Goldberg for introducing me to Joanne.

I owe my gratitude to two other irreplaceable friends: First and foremost, my long-time co-conspirator, photographer Mark Lohman, for always being ready to embark on new projects. Though our schedule is often insane, you always deliver, never complain and, without fail, make the work fun and relax. Finally, to my multi-talented friend Sunday Hendrickson for her photography of two of the charming homes (Organically Grown and Rural Romance) featured in this book.

With love and appreciation to all.
Fifi O'Neill